ISBN: 9798673815595 4th edition

Get to YES!

Idea-rich introductions to the subtle art of creative persuasion in sales and negotiation

"When you want to convert someone to your point of view, you go over to where he is standing, take him by the hand (mentally speaking), and guide him. You don't call him dummy; you don't order him to come over to where you are. You start where he is, and work from that position. That's the only way to get him to budge." Thomas Aquinas

By Bob 'Idea Man' Hooey
Author, "Think Beyond the FIRST Sale"

"To get to the Promised Land, you need to negotiate your way through the wilderness." Herb Cohen

Problems are a part of life and even more so of being in business. Problems may be why you exist in business. How you view them and deal with them is a pivot point for your long-term profitability and even sales survival.

What problems do you and your products or services solve for your clients? How can you make sure they know what you offer to help them make their lives, homes, and businesses better or easier? **This is 'why' they buy from you!**

Table of contents

"Always do your best. What you plant now, you will harvest later." **Og Mandino**

Chapter 1: A word as we begin…

If you want to be consistently successful and persuasive in the sales or negotiation process you need <u>only</u> understand and <u>apply</u> some simple ideas. Make it simple, keep your focus, and work through to a positive result that works for all parties.

As a sales professional and/or negotiator:

- **You will be more effective** when you are sensitive and aware of the real needs, motivation, and position of your client.
- **You will be more powerful**, when you are clear about your own needs, motivation, position, and what you bring to the table.
- **You will be more persuasive** when you learn to actively listen and state your case with clarity and confidence.

In preparing for the updating of this book I have drawn from many sources, hastily scribbled notes from seminars, articles, as well as drawing from a few of the books I've previously penned. I include the information here as a resource for you. We have not attempted to cite in the electronic text all the authorities and sources consulted in the preparation of this manual. To do so would require much more space than is available.

As mentioned earlier, this book is not intended to be a definitive piece, simply one person's experience, mine.

We need to explore ways of being more effective with our time which will free up our energy and resources for our most important goal - finding, negotiating with, selling, and retaining our clients. Perhaps these ideas will help you in that regard.

Sales and negotiation are a core part of building long term mutually profitable relationships. To be effective in sales and business, you must deal with three areas.

- **Pain**
- **Gain**
- **Sustaining**

To the degree that you work with your clients to take care of these areas your profitability and long-term viability will be impacted. Each area has its specific focus and profit center.

If we help people deal with their **pain** - will they need us when it's gone? Helping them to **gain** offers a bit more opportunity to serve. But if you can work with them through the pain, help them gain, and then take them through to helping them grow and **sustain** growth you will become a major part of their team.

Keep your eye on a mutually acceptable win for you and your client. Keep your eye on the long-term mutually profitable relationship if you want to succeed and stay profitable.

"If you're not taking care of your customers, your competitor will!"
Bob 'Idea Man' Hooey

#2 on Brian Tracy's Top 30 Motivational Sales Quotes for Success

Chapter 2: Principles on Power Negotiating Techniques

In the negotiation process - a critical part of the sale process - it is imperative to understand the basic principles that help make the top sales professionals/negotiators so successful. In addition to understanding these principles we need to learn how and when to apply them.

We negotiate everyday: with our family and friends, our co-workers to cover for us, with our employers for salaries and perks, our suppliers to support us, and with our clients for sales.

Following these basic principles will enable you to negotiate intelligently and fairly, which will, in turn, increase the chances of arriving at a win-win resolution. Fine tuning your negotiating skills will secure you a more profitable and sustainable sales career and company.

These points will assist you in becoming a powerful negotiator, better equipped in the sales and negotiation process.

If you are **client-oriented** sales professional who plans on being here for the long term, you understand that it is better to focus on how both you and the client can win.

Regardless of what you want, in the end, the **other person must be satisfied** - or at least feel satisfied - with what they got.

Separate the people from the obstacle inhibiting a mutually satisfying conclusion.

Focus on solving problems and not on the emotions arising from the problem. Don't make or take it personally. Look for the best solution to help both parties win!

Knowing the **negotiation style** of the person you are negotiating with is critical to leaving with a positive outcome for both parties.

Focus on interests, not your positions. Positions can be fixed. Each of you may have interests which need to be met. Fixed, inflexible items can put your negotiations into a corner and a stalemate. There may be areas on which you can meet on common ground or agree to creatively compromise.

Keep your emotions in check. **Never fall in love with something.** Doing so puts you at risk of losing some of your chips in the game. Don't over-react or get angry. It's not about winning. It's about **arriving at a mutual win.**

Actively listen to and (probe) question the person you are negotiating with. You may discover a better deal than you ever thought possible.

These principles, when properly applied, will dramatically increase your chances of successfully concluding your negotiations; which means that both (all) parties walk away with an agreement deemed satisfactory. If you are committed to **gaining repeat business**, this needs to be the focus and the foundation of your sales negotiation and follow-up relationship.

Think Beyond The First Sale by www.SuccessPublications.ca goes into this in greater depth. Get your copy now.

These success principles apply equally in both personal and professional situations requiring negotiation. They can assist you in having more satisfying relationships and an even more profitable career path. **Apply them wisely and fairly.**

Chapter 3: Traits of the 'effective' sales professional or negotiator

Believe it or not, there are some traits that will help you in being more effective in the sales and negotiation game. Some of these are learned; most are based on your character as evidenced by your day-to-day actions.

Doesn't need to be liked: The effective sales professional or negotiator is there to do their job and reach the best result possible given the situation, the timing, and those in the process. They are not out to deliberately upset anyone; but they are also not there just to be friendly. It's not about friendship but on-going service and mutually beneficial relationships.

Able to tolerate conflict and ambiguity: The role of the negotiator is to navigate between conflict with other parties, positions, and policies. Often, things are very ambiguous, and the role of the effective negotiator is to help clarify and move on to a successful mutually acceptable conclusion.

Integrity: This is the bedrock characteristic of the truly effective negotiator. This is where you built long-term mutually beneficial client relationships.

No need to be the 'smartest' person in the room: Enough said.

Regards everything as negotiable: This is the 'sales-game' and everything is subject to discussion and decision in the process. Ok, perhaps not everything, e.g. morals and legalities; but almost everything else is open to be discussed.

Good people sense: This is where the true sales professional or negotiator shines. They know how to read people and they know how to work with them to reach a mutually acceptable result.

Strong competitive streak: They like to win, to create a good deal for everyone.

Big picture mentality: This is where they do well in keeping their eye on the larger picture, the best result and not allowing themselves to get bogged down or distracted by small details that do not move the deal forward.

Eye for crucial detail: Having said the above, they are particularly good at seeing the crucial details in any discussion. Perhaps details the other negotiation team has overlooked that proved the edge or leverage to get the deal to completion.

Patience: They have learned to work for the long-term and allow the process to evolve. Sometimes that tries their patience, but they keep it and that gives them an edge.

Clarity: They can keep focused and clear on the job at hand and the deal in the future. They don't allow themselves to let outside influences cloud their judgement or their insights.

Mastery of the details: In sales and negotiation, the mastery is 'in' the details. They are conscious of all the relevant details that impact the eventual completion of their deal. They make sure they are handled well. This is a foundation for long-term client relationships.

Administrative skills: They track details, discussions, and all relevant points of the project or deal being negotiated. They want it to be right and to work correctly once completed.

Give each of these traits a moment of thought…

- Do you agree with it as a trait for a good sales professional or negotiator?
- Do you disagree? Why?
- Do you see any of these traits that you already possess?
- Are there some you can enhance, learn, or apply?
- When will you start?
- What do you need to change?

Chapter 4: Active Listening is a Master Skill used by powerful negotiators

Successful negotiators are often 'master' listeners. In fact, they work hard at being good listeners.

They listen to what people are saying, how they are saying it, and at times what they 'aren't' saying. They use their enhanced listening skills to give them an edge in the negotiation. Listening provides an intuitive edge that allows them to more effectively negotiate and to get a better result.

Active listening is rarely taught in schools because many educators (along with almost everyone else) erroneously assume listening is tantamount to breathing -- automatic. Everyone does it, but few do it well. *(Bob taught an active listening skills course at Langara College in Vancouver for several years.)*

Effective listening is a learned skill. Like any other skill, competency in listening is only achieved through learning and practice. The scarcity of good listeners is self- perpetuating. If you didn't have good listeners to learn from and (especially) models to emulate, you probably didn't master this 'master' skill. Instead, many learned whatever ***passed*** for listening in your environment: distracted half-attention, constant interruptions, multi-layered, high-volume, talk-fest free-for-alls with little listening at all.

Barriers to Active Listening

Effective listening takes time or, more bluntly, you have to invest the time to actually listen. **Too often we are too busy to listen.**

A life programmed with back-to-back commitments offers little leeway for active listening. Similarly, a mind constantly buzzing with plans, dreams, schemes, and anxieties is difficult to keep clear. Good listening requires the temporary suspension of all unrelated thoughts to allow focus.

Focus! To become an effective listener, you have to learn to manage what goes on in your own mind. Technology, for all its gifts, has erected new barriers to listening. Face-to-face meetings and telephone conversations (listening opportunities) are to often being replaced by email and the sterile anonymity of electronic meeting rooms, or zoom calls. Meanwhile television and the internet continue to capture or divert countless hours that might otherwise be available for conversation, dialogue, and listening.

Other barriers to active listening include:

…worry, fear, anger, grief, and depression
…individual bias and prejudice
…semantics and language differences
…noise and verbal "clutter"
…preoccupation, boredom, and shrinking attention spans

Listening Out Loud – Active vs. passive

A good listener is not just a silent receptacle, passively receiving the thoughts and feelings of others. To be an effective listener, you must respond with verbal and nonverbal cues which let the speaker know that you are listening and understanding. You must respond to draw out the full intent of your speaker in your quest to listen and understand. These responses are typically called feedback.

Verbal feedback works best when delivered in the form of brief statements, rather than questions. Your questions usually get answered if you wait. Statements allow you to paraphrase and reflect on what you've heard, which affirms the speaker's success at communicating and encourages the speaker to elaborate further or delve more deeply into the topic. Meaningful exchanges and real dialogue are built on feedback.

To accurately feed back a person's thoughts and feelings, you have to be consciously, actively engaged in the process of listening. Hearing a statement, you create a mental model, experiencing or visualizing what the speaker is describing, feeling the speaker's feelings through the filters of your own humanity and experience.

Ten Steps to Effective Listening

- Face the speaker and maintain eye contact. Don't stare.
- Be attentive yet relaxed.
- Keep an open mind.
- Listen to the words and try to create a picture of what the speaker is saying.
- Don't interrupt and don't impose your 'solutions'.
- Wait for the speaker to pause to ask clarifying questions.
- Ask questions only to ensure understanding of something that has been said (avoiding questions that disrupt the speaker's train of thought).
- Try to feel what the speaker is feeling.
- Give the speaker regular feedback, e.g., summarize, reflect feelings, or simply say "uh huh".
- Pay attention to what *isn't said* -- to feelings, facial expressions, gestures, posture, and other nonverbal cues.

Someone told me once that, "Listening is a precious gift - the gift of time."

It helps build relationships, solve problems, ensure better understanding, resolve conflicts, and improve accuracy. At work, effective listening means fewer errors and less wasted time. At home, it helps develop resourceful, self-reliant kids who can solve their own problems. It helps build better relationships too. In the sales process it is the forgotten secret. Listening builds friendships and careers. It saves money and marriages. It is the forgotten communication skill; but it can be learned.

More Listening Tips

Mentally screen out distractions, like background activity and noise. Try not to focus on the speaker's accent or speech mannerisms to the point where they become distractions. Finally, don't be distracted by your own thoughts, feelings, or biases.

- When listening for long stretches, focus on (and remember) key words and issues.
- When dealing with difficult people, spend more time listening than speaking.
- When in doubt about whether to listen or speak, keep listening.

Learn to Listen is available from www.SuccessPublications.com and covers this learnable skill in more depth.

Chapter 5: Learning their patterns

As you deal with people over time, you begin to understand how they negotiate and scope out the regular patterns or tactics they employ. If you have studied the typical patterns people use, you will have created proactive strategies to effectively deal with them and move forward to a successful negotiation.

Understanding is the beginning of being able to negotiate effectively.

Here are four typical patterns:

Concession pattern: Always looking for a concession or reduction. Often, this is their opening negotiation ploy. They want you to give something away, without getting anything in return. **Don't do it!** Always look for a trade off, this is how you create a win-win!

Poor mouth pattern: Always complaining about how poor they are or how bad things are… want you to feel sorry for them. Don't fall for it. You are not in business for charity. You need to be able to productively serve your clients. **Profit** is not a bad word; more so if you want to stay in business long enough to serve them.

Splitting the difference pattern: This one seems to be logical, at first. Let's just agree to split the difference. However, this is seldom fair and equitable for both sides when you check into the real costs and investments. Know your real costs, profits, and what you have to discuss. Stay focused on the real costs in the process and where your profit lies.

Adding to the deal (accession) pattern: Here they want you to throw something else (free) into the mix after you have a deal. Something that costs you money. Be very careful here, as this can easily make this a win-lose for you and your company. Everything has its price and you need to remain vigilant.

Similarly, some other **stumbling blocks** come up to make negotiation difficult. Learning to block these tactics are essential to being effective and getting the detail, to working through to a successful agreement.

You don't have to accept a negative attack: This is business as well as personal space. Don't allow anyone to treat you badly or be negative in your direction. Keep focused and keep positive and be willing to stop negotiations.

You don't have to accept an ultimatum: Never accept a deal when it is a take it or leave it proposition or reinforced with undue pressure. Remember, the only good deal is one that is good for all parties. **Know when to say no and walk away.** No when to take them off your client list too.

Side-step the 'bulk order': This can too often be a ploy… give us this special price, service, etc. and we'll give you a larger order down the road. This often is a scam and a way to pry money from your kids' mouths, or your retirement plans. Offer to give them a rebate on future orders based on a volume discount produced or delivered. This can work in your favor if you position it correctly.

Don't give the other side an easy out: This is where 'poor' salespeople and negotiators leave money and deals on the table. You came to make a deal – make the deal. Deal with them fairly and allow enough time to decide.

Don't be afraid to give them a reasonable time factor for what you are offering and stick to it.

When I was designing kitchens and gave a price quote it was only good for a limited time. Prices and availability of materials can change, and I reserved the right to re-quote later if they delayed. Integrity is saying what you mean and meaning what you say.

If what you are offering is a time sensitive offer, say so and mean it. *I remember one year working for a large kitchen design company who had a special on orders including a free countertop. I worked until almost midnight on the last day processing orders. Orders that were only good for the free top when received at the manufacturing plant by midnight.*

Don't fall for the old 'good cop/bad cop' routine: Remember all the cop and spy shows where they play the perp against two cops: One plays the really bad nasty cop who intimidates them and the second comes on as a more reasonable friendly type to get them to open up. I've seen negotiators try this ploy. See it for what it is and deal with it upfront. When you see this, be sure you want to play or just walk away.

Chapter 6: Negotiation in sales

Here are some tips that will help you prepare to effectively negotiate from a position of strength and be proactive and strategic in your action. **Negotiate to win – but first, prepare yourself to win!**

Negotiation sales tips

Have a list of demands or base points prepared in advance: Know going in what your points of negotiation are and aren't.

Knowledge equates to power: The more you know about yourself and your competition the better position you are in to make a better, informed deal.

Price is only one criterion: Remember there are many factors that make a deal worthy. Money invested is only one of them. Don't get sidetracked on the dollars. Look at the 'full deal' and all its aspects and details. Then decide if you want the deal.

Aim higher: Don't be afraid to go for a better deal right from the beginning. The inexperienced negotiator or salesperson is the one who is the first to settle for a lower deal or concede.

Use your time patiently: Don't rush into the deal. Make time to discuss and scope out all the areas on the table. Don't be impatient, that usually ends up with you walking away with a lesser deal.

Invoke legitimacy: Make sure you are dealing with legitimate or real issues, not just those invented by the other side to side-track you. Deal with the straw man or false point early.

Use funny money or 'soft dollars': It's not about money. It might be about other areas where you can make adjustments. For example, payment terms, storage, extra service, deliveries, or warranties.

Negotiate the non-negotiable: Everything is open for discussion. Don't be afraid to ask!

Use your ears - applied listening skills: Your ears can be a secret weapon if you know what to listen for. Often your opponent will reveal more than they should.

Scope out the buyer's position early: Find out what they are willing to trade, how far they are willing to go, what they can live with and what they can't live without. Apply that knowledge.

Flip the iceberg: What is under the surface. Bring it up as a part of the discussion. Often your opponents want to keep it surface based where they control the agenda and the terms of the negotiation. Lead the negotiation – win the negotiation.

"Lagniappe" - a little extra: Once you have completed your deal, why not give them something extra as a way of saying thank you. After all, you are looking for a long term mutually profitable relationship, aren't you? Decide in advance what this might be and make sure you can afford it.

When I was designing kitchens, I always built a little 'flex' into my quotes. That way, when we were installing the project I could accommodate the clients with little changes without extra billing. Made for happier clients when they got something extra.

Know which areas are available for negotiation. Know the full scope of what you can negotiate and where to draw the line. Make sure you cover the full costs of each decision.

- **Negotiation Areas**
- **Specifications change**
- **Drop shipment**
- **Terms**
- **Increased volume**
- **Longer commitment**
- **Additional items**
- **Freight and delivery**
- **Referrals**
- **Packaging change**

Discounting

Be careful when you discount or make major concessions. It can cost you big time (profits, actual costs) down the road if you don't know the full impact of your discounts. Here are some areas to watch.

- **Time limit**
- **Negotiate individually**
- **Don't set precedents**
- **Get more down the road**
- **Watch your image**
- **Don't compound decisions**
- **Carefully consider the increase in sales**
- **Know when to discount**

Again, we are going to allow you to dig deeper and learn the concepts behind each of these. When you dig deep you will learn them and then be better prepared to use them appropriately. Invest in a good sales book to learn more.

Chapter 7: Mistakes Made by Newer Sales Staff

One of the areas where newer sales staff struggle is in their negotiation during the sales process. They don't listen as well, they aren't as prepared, and often they fail to ask for the order.

Why is it that some senior or seasoned sales staff are often more effective and productive in their sales efforts?

Why are some sales staff better at building long-term, profitable relationships that result in repeat sales and multiple referrals?

Could it be that they've learned these simple points that help them connect, negotiate, sell better and build more profitable client relationships?

As we have previously discussed, companies and selling professionals that take good care of their clients generally retain them for an extended period. For ineffective sales staff or newer sales personnel who lack the proper training, there are some **pitfalls here as well:**

Lack of preparation. Someone once said that **"Success happens when opportunity meets preparedness."**

Your level of preparedness directly impacts your credibility with a client and can make or break the establishment of a trust relationship. This means knowing your product or service as well as your firm's policies and procedures. It also means having a good understanding of what your competition provides in these same areas. **Prepare yourself to win** and work diligently to make sure you become a trusted advisor in your client dealings.

Why is it we feel we can simply go through our life and our careers winging it or going with the flow? Why is it so few invest the time to prepare themselves to win, to grow, and to succeed?

Not listening. 90% of salespeople never listen or listen ineffectively and are subsequently doomed to frustration and lack of success in their selling activities. **Active listening** is the key foundation to discovering your client's current and future needs and to determining your ability to meet them. **Asking questions and listening carefully** through the interview or qualification part of the conversation is where you build solid foundations for later sales success.

*I remember being interviewed by a national Canadian magazine on sales and being asked many questions about closing, overcoming objections, and such. As I recall, I told the interviewer that, **"…most of the situations they presented (examples mentioned by the interviewer) could be dealt with by more effective qualifying. Ask probing questions earlier in the sales conversation and listen to what your clients tell you. Their answers will provide the guidance you need to help them make effective buying decisions."***

Failing to ask for the order. This is the most critical part of your sales conversation. Yet, most of the studies I've read show that 70% of all salespeople <u>never</u> ask for the order. A larger percentage never asks for additional orders. Do you?

I remember asking a group of home furnishing salespeople in Wisconsin, **"Would you like to learn how to double or even triple your sales income in the next year?"** Hands went up across the auditorium. I paused for dramatic effect and told them the secret, **"Simply ask for the order at least twice in the sales conversation."** I went on to say, **"Most of you are not asking even once!"** One of their leading sales ladies told me afterwards that I was right on the money.

Poor or no follow up. Follow up and follow through is where 90% of all great sales are made. Conversely, this is where the majority of sales staff miss the opportunity to gain and maintain a client. This is where the real sale begins, and the relationship is built for long-term profitability.

I am continually surprised at how few salespeople follow up on leads or even make a minimal effort to keep in touch with current clients. A simple act of keeping in touch could provide the leverage to a long and mutually beneficial and profitable relationship. ***Think referrals!***

Small thinking. Want bigger sales? You must think and act bigger. Ask these questions: "How high is too high? What is my maximum potential? What is the lifetime value of my relationship with this client? What is the potential for referrals from this client?"

Think big and act accordingly to see your sales results soar. Dream it and then move confidently ahead to create foundations under your dreams.

Failing to establish and/or maintain rapport. This can be a killer if you have any aspirations of maintaining a mutually profitable relationship over a long period of time with your clients.

Investing time, at the beginning of your sales conversation, is crucial to your long-term success. Building on that rapport by keeping in touch can separate you from the lacklustre salespeople in your field. It will also help attract clients who will become active cheerleaders and champions on your behalf.

Failing to commit and establish one's self as an expert in your field. People like to deal with (and talk about) people who know what they are doing. Failing to present yourself as such negatively impacts or restricts your future earnings with clients.

Do your homework so you know your products, your services, and your industry. People love to work with people who know what they are doing and who earn their trust by their demonstrated expertise and credibility. A bit of study now can make a major difference in your future earnings and success.

Ask yourself how you fare in each of these above areas:

- Would you give yourself a passing mark?
- Which areas need a little work?
- How will you change what you do to make sure you give your clients the most professional service possible?

If you are in management, give your sales team a chance to win by reminding them of these success tactics. Remind them to keep focused and keep working toward their goals of helping the client make a decision that is both good for the client and profitable over the long haul for the company.

How can you change and/or help your sales team make the changes necessary to become a professional salesperson/team and provide continued value-added service?

Chapter 8: Would you buy from yourself?

Conducting an image self-evaluation

"Perception is reality!" This is often the case in business dealings. People still like to deal with people they like or trust. Ask yourself it this is true in your own selection of people you do business with overall.

People base their business perceptions on the image we portray. That image is enhanced or blurred by how we act or present ourselves. This is very crucial in negotiation. This is especially true when looking at the factors that influence people to do business with us on a repeat basis. We may be able to *'sell'* them once; but how do we ensure they continue wanting to deal with us? **Think referrals and repeat orders!**

Take a moment and give some honest feedback to yourself, based on your past 6 months experience in dealing with your clients, colleagues, and suppliers.

Hint: The answers here might show you where you can improve your service to gain and retain clients! Your answers might also reveal weaknesses that will hurt you as you attempt to negotiate. Discuss your answers with your fellow sales staff, clients, and employees so everyone learns.

- Is your image one of honesty and straightforward sincerity? How do you know?
- From the buyer's point of view, would you be considered reliable? Why is that true?
- Could you honestly say your customers received special benefits dealing with you not available from one of your competitors? What? Why?
- In their eyes, would you appear to be an expert in your field? Why would they say that?
- Have you been effective in helping solve their problems? How so?
- Would you say you handled complaints to their complete satisfaction? How? Share some examples.
- Is **'integrity'** one of your watchwords? How does it show in your dealings?
- Other than your business dealings, would you think your clients believe you have their best interests and welfare at heart? Why?
- Do clients look at you as a good reliable source of product or service information? Why?
- Would the majority of your clients continue dealing with your business, even if a competitor offered slightly lower prices? Why would they do that?
- What percentage of your new clients comes from referrals? Why is that number significant? What can you do to enhance this form of client generation?
- How do you plan to keep yourself and your staff educated and current in your field? Where will you invest in your future and profitability? (Hire me! ☺)
- Describe how you keep in touch with past clients. Describe the results.

If you have been honest in your appraisal of your actions and business operations, you might have seen a few areas in which improvement would help.

Go back over your answers and ask yourself:

- How can I improve how I service and seek my clients?
- How can I change what I offer them to reflect more accurately what they need?
- How can I make a difference in my career and my community by making the changes I see needed here?
- How can I equip my staff and co-workers to better reflect the changes needed?
- How can I partner with other business owners to strengthen and expand the way we do business and the services or products we deliver?
- How can you reorganize your business to allow you to enjoy your life better?

Honest reflection, followed by a commitment to act, will perform miracles.

Time and time again sales professionals have done some soul searching and come up with some great ways to re-invent their business and give their clients the long-term service they deserve!

The game of sales and negotiation is best played with enthusiasm and openness. The successful sale professional or negotiator is one who is always *'on-the-grow'*, and on the look out for ways to do it better. Are you?

Chapter 9: Reasons Why People Buy and Keep on Buying

In his excellent book, **"Rapid Response Advertising"** Geoff Ayling provides sales professionals with fifty reasons why people buy. Knowing 'why' people make purchases will allow you to position and continually re-position yourself and your company to help them do so. This knowledge will give you an edge to gain them and in retaining them as long-term clients and repeat buyers. This knowledge will assist you in being more effective in your negotiations and in winning their trust and business.

One of our Ideas At Work facilitators discusses his top 25 reasons people buy in his **Make ME Feel Special - client service - business success program**. *He contends that we increase our ability to serve and sell our clients when we see our products and services through their eyes. He challenges his participants to see how many reasons they can give their prospective clients to buy from them… and keep on buying. www.ideaman.net*

See how many of Geoff's fifty reasons already align or fit with your product and service offerings. Discuss how you might adapt, amend, adapt, or add on to what you currently offer to make yourself a more attractive resource for meeting your client's needs over a longer period.

This is one of the secrets of getting repeat business: give your client a valid reason to do so! How about 50 plus reasons!

People make purchases for these, among other reasons:

- To make more money
- To become more comfortable
- To attract praise
- To increase enjoyment
- To possess things of beauty
- To avoid criticism
- To make their work easier
- To speed up their work
- To keep up with the Joneses
- To feel opulent
- To look younger
- To become more efficient
- To buy (some just like to shop)
- To avoid effort
- To escape or avoid pain
- To protect their possessions
- To be in style
- To avoid trouble
- To access opportunities
- To express love
- To be entertained
- To be organized
- To feel safe
- To conserve energy
- To be accepted
- To save time
- To become more fit and healthy
- To attract the opposite sex
- To protect their family
- To emulate others
- To protect their reputation

- To feel superior
- To be trendy
- To be excited
- To communicate better
- To preserve the environment
- To satisfy an impulse
- To save money
- To be cleaner
- To be popular
- To gratify curiosity
- To satisfy their appetite
- To be individual
- To escape stress
- To gain convenience
- To be informed
- To give to others
- To feel younger
- To pursue a hobby
- To leave a legacy

Here is one more solid reason that motivates people to make a purchase: to avoid pain.

Thomas Jefferson said, ***"The art of life is the art of avoiding pain; and he is the best pilot, who steers clearest of the rocks and shoals with which it is beset."***

A few years back, Sam Deep and Lyle Sussman, who wrote **Close the Deal**, taught the importance of pain and the ways to learn where it resides. If you know exactly, you've got a great starting point for your creativity.

Now that you've got 50 plus ways to win the hearts and business of your prospects, you'll have an easier job of being an effective negotiator and in winning sales, repeat sales, and increased profits. Know why they decide, and you can negotiate from a position of strength.

I challenge you to go through each of these buying reasons with an eye to aligning them with specific aspects or benefits of your products or services. See if you can identify which emotions are in play when you are in the sales and negotiation process. Perhaps you will need to adapt what you offer to expand their reasons to do business with you. These are areas of interest and potential negotiation points to consider.

Chapter 10: What is your deal? What do they want?

What does your client need or really want?

This is an opening point to a successful negotiation. Knowing what is important to your client provides guidance as you initiate discussion that leads to a successful decision.

It is important to understand the difference between your clients wants and needs. **Often, wants are often the impulses that incite their needs.**

Client Needs

Client needs generally share the following characteristics:

- **Rational** – they are rational, and it makes sense to satisfy them as they relate to the client's career, living conditions, health, financial success, appearance, or whichever issue your product addresses.
- **Top of mind** – they exist as a top of mind or surface image for your clients. They are aware of them and can discuss them openly with you.
- **Fact-oriented** – needs are a matter of fact. They are not based on theory or conjecture but in reality. An intelligent analysis of the client's situation will unearth them for discussion.

Client Wants

Client wants are quite different from client needs:

- **Emotional** – wants are personal and emotional. They are independent of your product and service. Clients carry them around like baggage.
- **Below the surface** – clients don't often reveal their wants easily. As a professional salesperson, you have to dig below the surface to help unearth them.
- **Perception-oriented** – rather than being fact oriented (like needs), wants are tied into a client's perception. As professional salespeople we have to tap into our client's wants and create an emotional bond that helps make the sale.

The effective negotiator learns to identify and differentiate between their client's needs and their client's wants. During the negotiation process this information provides a solid edge in favour of the better negotiator.

Chapter 11: Rules of Value-Added Selling and Top-Level Service

Being a top-level successful salesperson is a **delicate** proposition in balancing client needs while maintaining your profitability. Following these rules of **value-added selling** and top-level service will give you a definitive edge over your completion.

Client satisfaction is relative to your actual or perceived performance and your client's expectations.

Client satisfaction is a very subjective thing to measure. It really is a matter of perception and experience. If you meet or exceed the unsaid, unwritten expectations of your clients, their perception will be a positive one. Fail to meet these expectations and you will find them less than satisfied.

One approach to ensure that you meet or beat these **unsaid —unwritten** expectations is to conduct research. Often, within an industry there are certain expectations which serve as the norm. Make sure you know what they are and use them as the bottom line in your service and performance. If you want to succeed in gaining repeat business and client loyalty, make sure you go well past their normal expectations.

There is some business you <u>don't</u> want; but value every opportunity to explore the potential of doing business.

When you first start in sales or business, you want to deal with everyone. This works for the short-term, but not over the long-term. As difficult as it seems, you need to fire some clients if the business they bring in is not profitable or is labour intensive to you or your company.

Studies have shown that on average, 80% of your business will be generated from 20% of your clients. Yet many sales staff continuously invest their time in those clients which bring the lowest return on their investment.

Trying to be all things to all people is a sure-fire way to go broke. You cannot effectively sell, service, or supply everyone. You need to decide early on **'what business you are really in'** and what you can provide profitably to your clients. This is even truer when you negotiate.

You cannot service them if you are no longer in business. Sales and its built-in client service is a long-term investment in your business.

Not all clients are valid targets for a value-added effort.

As you develop your business and sales, decide which clients you can service profitably. **Profit is not a bad word;** it is the lifeline of your business. Profit is what differentiates a job or hobby from a successful sales career.

As you become increasingly clear on **what business you are in** and what you can profitably provide in the marketplace, you will be better able to target and serve your clients. Selling when you are not able to do so profitably or service in a cost-effective way will detract from the potential you have to build your business. Simply put, if you haven't earned any profits, you have nothing to re-invest to expand your business.

Price is less important when the relationship between the buyer and the seller is strong.

Think about your own shopping or buying experiences:

- Other than for convenience or disposable goods, where do you shop on a regular basis? Why?
- Would you drive across town to save a few dollars?
- How often would you continue to deal with that company or salesperson even if they are a bit higher in price? Why is that?

When the value of your product and its support and service are evident, and there is a strong relationship built on understanding and trust, people tend to be loyal and will continue dealing with you.

Ask yourself…

- Would you agree that it is often the way you are treated that makes a big difference?
- Would you also agree that often it is the small details than make the difference?
- How can you develop this type of relationship with your clients?
- What would have to change to make it work in your situation?

One final question

How can you apply the lessons learned from your own shopping experience to improve that of your potential and existing clients?

"You don't need a big close as many sales reps believe. You risk losing your customer when you save all the good stuff for the end. Keep the customer actively involved throughout your presentation, and watch your results improve." **Harvey Mackay**

Chapter 12: Checkpoints for Super Sales Techniques

Here are a few check points to keep in mind as you enter or continue to work in the field of sales and negotiation. Please keep these checkpoints in mind, as they've been drawn from tactics used by successful salespeople in various fields. The most successful salespeople know how to take care of business, they know how to maximize their presentations, and they certainly know how to effectively negotiate.

If you are to be successful as a negotiator, as a sales professional, and/or in business, consider these your homework. When you have done your homework, you are more likely to get a passing grade and be successful in your endeavours. Most of these are self-evident; but I challenge you to give some thought to each one in how it is relevant to what you currently do. **Be informed – be successful.**

YOU and YOUR STAFF

Be neatly groomed
Smile sincerely
Keep the work area neat
Recognize the client immediately on entry to your location or in entering theirs

CARING

Be sincere
Use a greeting that requires a positive response
Focus on the client and the merchandise

Emphasize a desire to serve

LISTENING

Actively listen for the message behind the words
Be aware of the client's body language

TELEPHONE TIPS

Answer promptly and politely
Put a smile in your voice
Speak clearly
Personalize the conversation

ONLINE TIPS

Respond quickly and accurately
Personalize your communication
Ask qualifying questions to better serve them

MERCHANDISE

Know what merchandise or services you offer
Know where it is located
Know when it is available

BENEFITS/FEATURES

Listen to the client to find out what they consider to be product benefits or features
Sell the client the product benefit supplemented with the product features

SELLING

Demonstrate products using a "you" attitude
Differentiate between excuses and objections
Ask only positive questions when closing a sale
Suggest complementary merchandise

KNOW YOUR CLIENT or CUSTOMER

AIDA (attention, interest, desire, action)
LEAR (listening, empathizing, asking questions, responding)
Use "what" questions

Remember you are always negotiating and selling. **The sale only starts when the client says yes!**

Your company, its reputation, your services and guarantees, your selection and product mix, your staff expertise and friendliness, your ability to solve my problems, and your willingness to go the extra mile to see that I am satisfied.

What changes do you need to make to make sure you meet and surpass these checkpoints?

"To build a long-term, successful enterprise, when you don't close a sale, open a relationship." Patricia Fripp

Chapter 13: Proactive strategies to 'minimize' price objections

How do you successfully compete when you know you aren't the **least expensive** in your area or industry? How do you compete in an increasingly competitive market globally? How do you compete with a big box store opening in your neighbourhood? **Here are some areas that will help you in this regard. Remember, it is not always about the money. Always about perceived value for the investment.**

Strategic Value Analysis: Taking the time to find out a bit about these four areas will help you build a strong foundation and relationship to better service your customers. Better relationships will take the pressure of the price factor in the buying decision. The more you know, the better you can apply that knowledge in serving those who need what you provide.

- **Market Analysis**
- **Competitive Analysis**
- **Self-analysis**
- **Customer analysis**

Positioning Strategies - to create barriers: Some of the more successful companies have carved out a position as the quality leader in their field. This emphasis on *'quality or value'* moves the evaluation process away from price comparisons.

Outsmart the competition: Use your brains and look for ways to better 'service' your customers. Find ways to provide services or value-added products that your competition doesn't.

Use all your resources: Being lean and mean in using your resources can help you keep your overhead in line and keep your pricing competitive. Using your resources fully allows you to better serve as well.

Decide on all organizational needs: Taking time to streamline your operation. Keep it simple! This will help your staff provide the best service possible. It also allows your customers to see firsthand your commitment to giving them value for their dollar.

Work to generate end-user support: If you are in the position of being a supplier, your customers are really your customers' customers. How can you help your customers by working to reach and teach the end users? Become a drawing point for your customers.

Value-added Checklist (10 minimum - go for 20)

Bundling: How about making what you offer more valuable by combining products or services to allow your customers lots of options? What types of bundles can you offer? Perhaps you can negotiate a better price for a combination package.

Proactive probing: Take time to find out what moves your customers. What keeps them up at night? Ask questions and respond to what you learn, by adapting or changing your business. This is one way of keeping what you offer current, valuable, and viable.

Reinforce value: Everything you do should be focused on reinforcing the value in what you offer. What is the true value of what you offer? Warranty, service, selection, delivery, options? What do you offer that brings more value to the table?

Sell intangibles: Often the true value of what you sell is based on things that can't be shown or proven until needed, as above. Do you have a better warranty? Do you offer better terms? Do you offer a better selection or stocking? Do you offer expert advice or consulting? Do you offer delivery and installation? **If so, let them know!**

Presentation ideas: When you get an opportunity to present or share about your business or products – I'd suggest looking for ways to incorporate the following areas. You can be a great spokesman if you do.

How can you…?

- Demonstrate earnings
- Cut their costs (investments)
- Go for agreement to product first
- Carefully choose your words
- Use proper sales terms instead of jargon
- Sandwich the price - focus on value (good, better, best!)
- Price with benefits summary
- Cost as a 'mere' fraction
- Minimize the cost-to-own
- Analogize
- Use testimonials wherever possible
- Think and talk *'long-term'*
- Present in its best light

The above critical *'impact'* areas are essential to being a value-based, sales and service business. Look for ways to build them into your business. **If you have strong competition, even more so!**

Using some of these tools and techniques can allow you to selectively compete and excel as you negotiate for their business. **The effort will pay off – BIG TIME!**

Chapter 14: Dealing with PRICE objections

If you are dealing with a situation or competitor where price becomes a major issue here are a few ideas that might jog your mind in preparation. I'd suggest buying a good sales book and boning up on the basic sales success techniques. *(Hint: invest in 'Think Beyond the FIRST Sale')*

However, if you make sure what you offer is **not perceived as a commodity**, you will have less of a challenge with price-based competitors. In the case of a commodity-based perception price is the key. Moving away from being perceived in that commodity category is a value-based activity.

Getting your clients to see the value makes the financial decision easier.

Here are a few tips for handling objections when they come up, and they will.

- Separate your ego from the sale – it is not about you – it is about helping them.

- Build a possible objections file and be able to answer them quickly and honestly.
- Positive anticipation of objections – deal with objections during your presentation
- Assist the client in saving face – sometimes they really can't buy from you.
- Listen with ALL your senses – look and listen to draw them out.
- Persistence pays off – don't back off simply because they raise an objection. The true professional knows he or she may have to negotiate a number of no's to **get to the yes.**

Three-step objections model

- **Clarify** – let me see if I understand this…
- **Buffer** – share some information that buffers the objection
- **Answer their objection** with a return to benefit-based statements.

Answering **PRICE** objections using some of these standard sales techniques. **Here is where you dig into your sales library to learn how each of these techniques work; and where it might be best used.** I decided to not spell them out for you. I believe when you research them you are more likely to understand the concept behind them. When you do, you become better prepared to negotiate and to win. One or several of them might be effective tool for negotiation in a sales situation. Having more tools allows you to be more productive and valuable to potential clients.

- Use the subtraction method
- Don't be afraid to cast doubt

- Reinforce the quality
- Ask hypothetical questions
- Go for the trial close
- Draw buyer's attention away from price
- Sell and build loyalty
- Share success stories
- Risk of 'cheapness'
- Work on buying dissonance
- Reverse tactic
- Alternate-advantage overload
- Competition to meet standards
- Future order
- Bottom line response

Three common price objections – and how to counter them. Professionals in this business have taken the time to look at their products or services and to become knowledgeable in answering questions concerning the benefits, features, policies, and procedures. **Invest time to figure out the common objections you might encounter and have a solid answer for each of them.**

Similarly, they have taken the time to think through their response to the following basic objections.

- **I don't have the money (budget)**
- **I can buy it cheaper somewhere else**
- **I don't see your value**

So how would you respond when a prospect uses one of these objections? Your answer may just be the secret to your ongoing success in this field of sales. Again, if you haven't already worked out the answers to these typical objections,

I'd suggest investing in a good sales book. These will come up on a regular basis and need to be a core part of your conversation if you intend being successful in the sales game.

Chapter 15: Ways to get the most from negotiating via email or other venues

Every day, businesspeople are using email (and the internet) to help speed up the communication and the negotiation process. This creates new conflicts (misunderstandings) and challenges the traditional ways of face to face or over the telephone negotiating.

The most important strategy is to know **WHEN to use email,** and **WHEN to pick up the phone** or arrange a face to face (could be a zoom call) negotiation. Email negotiating can be powerful when you work with someone who can relate and communicate effectively via email, and it can be a disaster if the other party isn't comfortable with this medium. Also, if your email negotiating even begins to get a hint of negativity, or that you feel that you're being misunderstood or you can't understand the end outcome of the person you're negotiating with, by all means, pick up the phone and **BREAK EMAIL SILENCE by calling them.**

Age range: Businesspeople, who are between 20 to 40 years old, are more open and able to embrace and use email negotiating as par for the normal business day course. Whereas older businesspeople may resist or blow the deal off, if you're trying to use email to negotiate.

The tell-tale signs: Does the person you are negotiating with call you on the phone after each email you send instead of replying to it? Now, this is NOT true for all people, as I know many people in their 50's and 60's and 70's that do not resist change and love email, text, or messenger. It might be a good hint to their preference.

LEVERAGE the power of email to ask questions you might feel squeamish to ask in real life. Dig deeper for other areas of common interest and speak to the ego of the person you are negotiating with. Praise his or her works or efforts, and most of all, be humble via email if you want to get the highest return on your time. You'd be surprised at what you can draw out of a person via email that you might not get in a face to face or telephone conversation. We're not talking trickery here; we're talking about taking a genuine interest in the other person via email. Get them to talk more about themselves and ASK open ended questions.

Use emoticons to develop a friendly email relationship. :-), ;-), :/, :-|, and so forth. You can also develop a stronger rapport with someone you've never meant, by just taking an interest in their special interests via an email discussion. You can even add video and audio greetings to your email now… search the web for apps. Do this selectively, don't over use.

Once you've found out a bit of their interests, why not send them URL's or gifts of information that might add value to their lives. This has helped to open folks up to better understand the kind of person you are and be more receptive to negotiating via email. Again, this is from the perspective of giving.

Take a look at yourself. Are you limiting the size of deal that you can negotiate via email? I'm here to tell you, that you can do multi million dollar deals nearly 95%+ via email, because I know people who have done it.

For many, negotiating via email is not about negotiating via email, but rather, it's just picking the communication that is the fastest to get the job done, with the outcome that you're after.

Using time to negotiate via email: Sometimes, not replying quickly can be used to indicate disinterest by you. But don't be caught in not replying quickly to the point where the other party feels like you don't care, and they need to move on. A fast response can indicate that you are either respecting their time and want to help move the deal along because it's important to you, or it can also mean that you want this deal MORE than they do; which is why you respond within minutes instead of days...and it may weaken your position.

He/She who has the most information via email wins rule: Many times when negotiating via email, you can look at the headers of the email to learn about relationships, systems, vendors of choice, and other vital info that is the unspoken message that your email communicates. Use this to your advantage or to make conversation via email to learn more of each other. Be careful not to use this as a weapon, but more to show your interest in the other party.

Another hint: If the party you are negotiating with uses one of the free email services, they probably aren't worth your time. Real businesspeople do not use free email services that tack on tacky 2-3 line email ads at the bottom of the email.

Bonus: I find that almost all of my email negotiations involve me doing a WHOIS lookup via the internic: www.internic.net/whois.html to find out the owner of a domain and/or other relationship info. You owe it to yourself to get to know this resource.

Bonus #2: If you want to learn more about the personality, and special interests of the person you are dealing with check them out on Google, Facebook, LinkedIn and other social media sites. **Leverage social media to help you prepare.**

Note 2020: More recently with Covid-19 people have been learning to use online platforms such as Zoom to communicate and to conduct business. This will be a sales tool for your future. Learn to apply it well.

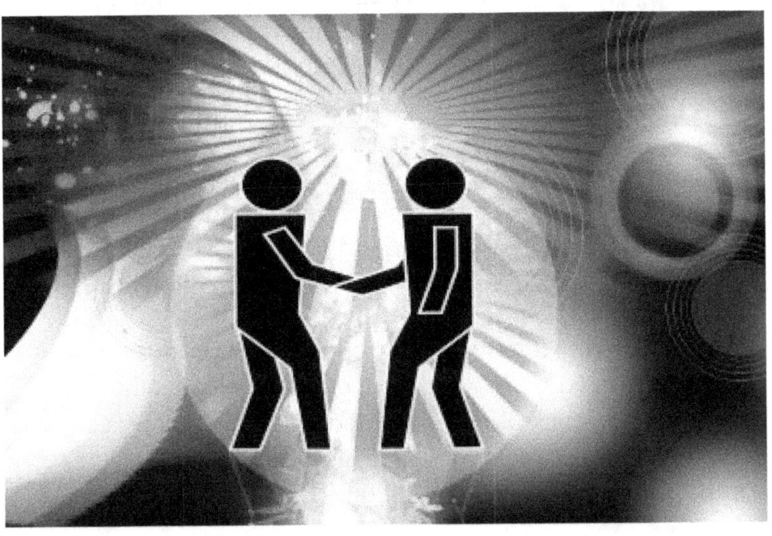

*We are working on a new book — **'Pivot to Present'** which will help equip you to effectively present virtually and this will help you sell online. It will be available from www.SuccessPublications.ca (Fall 2020)*

About the author

Bob 'Idea Man' Hooey is a charismatic, confident leader, corporate trainer, facilitator, Emcee, prolific author, and global motivational keynote speaker on creativity, sales success, business innovation, and enhancing team performance.

Using personal stories drawn from rich experience, he challenges his audiences to engage his **Ideas At Work! - to act on what they hear**, with clear, innovative, building-blocks and field-proven success techniques to increase their effectiveness. Bob challenges them to hone specific 'success skills' critical to their personal and professional advancement.

Bob outlines real-life, results-based, innovative ideas personally drawn from 29 plus years of rich leadership experience in retail, sales, construction, small business, entrepreneurship, manufacturing, association, consulting, community service, and commercial management.

Bob's conversational, often humorous, professional, and sometimes provocative style continues to inspire and challenge his audiences across North America. Bob's motivational, innovative, challenging, and practical **Ideas At Work!** have been successfully applied by thousands of sales leaders and professionals across the globe. *(60 countries so far)*

Bob is a frequent contributor to North American consumer, corporate, association, trade, and on-line publications on leadership, sales success, employee motivation and training;

as well as creativity and innovative problem solving, priority and time management, and effective customer service. He is the inspirational author of 30 plus publications including print and e-books. Visit: **www.SuccessPublications.ca** for more information and to order your copies.

Retired, award winning kitchen designer, Bob Hooey, CKD-Emeritus was one of only 75 Canadian designers to earn this prestigious certification by the National Kitchen and Bath Association.

In December 2000, Bob was given a special CAPS National Presidential award **"for his energetic contribution to the advancement of CAPS and his living example of the power of one"** and was elected to the CAPS National Board. He has been recognized by the National Speakers Association for his leadership contributions.

Bob was a co-founder and past President of the CAPS Vancouver Chapter, served as President of the CAPS Edmonton Chapter, and is an honorary member of the CAPS Atlantic Chapter as well as an honorary founding member of the CAPS Saskatchewan Chapter. He is a member of the NSA-Arizona Chapter and active in the National Speakers Association, PSA Spain, VSAI, the Canadian Association of Professional Speakers, as well as the Global Speakers Federation.

In 1998, Toastmasters International recognized Bob **"for his professionalism and outstanding achievements in public speaking"**. That August in Palm Desert, California Bob became the 48th speaker in the world to be awarded this prestigious professional level honour as an Accredited Speaker. He has been inducted into their Hall of Fame on several other occasions for his leadership contributions.

Distinguished Toastmaster, Bob served as Region Advisor for 2018-2019 training District leaders around the globe.

Bob has been honoured by the United Nations Association of BC (1993) and received the CANADA 125 award (1992) for his ongoing contributions to the community.

In 1998, Bob joined 3 other men to sail a 65-foot gaff rigged schooner from Honolulu, Hawaii to Kobe, Japan, barely surviving a 'baby' typhoon enroute.

Bob loves to travel and his speaking and writing have allowed him to visit 60 countries so far. Perhaps your organization would like to bring Bob in to share a few ideas with your team. Visit: www.HaveMouthWillTravel.com for more information.

Engage Canadian, Bob 'Idea Man' Hooey and put his Ideas At Work for your group, convention or association.

Call +1-780-736-0009 to find out how you can unleash your team's sales potential now! **Engage Bob Live or in a Virtual format today!** bhooey@mcsnet.ca

Ok, I want your business! 😊 I would love the opportunity to explore how we might work together, and how some of my programs or consulting might be a benefit for you or your team.

Visit my web sites for more information on what I bring to the table, **www.ideaman.net** or **www.BobHooey.training**

What they say about Bob 'Idea Man' Hooey

I frequently travel across North America, and more recently around the globe, sharing my **Ideas At Work!**

With the advent of Covid-19 I pivoted to serve my clients online with virtual presentations. Now you can bring me in virtually.

I am fortunate to get feedback and comments from my audiences and colleagues. These comments come from people who have been touched, challenged, or simply enjoyed themselves in one of my sessions.

"I still get comments from people about your presentation. Only a few speakers have left an impression that lasts that long. You hit a spot with the tourism people." Janet Bell, Yukon Economic Forums

"Thank you, Bob, it is always a pleasure to see a true professional at work. You have made the name 'Speaker' stand out as a truism - someone who encourages people to examine their lives and adjust. The comments indicated you hit people right where it is important - in their hearts. Each of those in your audience took away a new feeling of personal success and encouragement." Sherry Knight, Dimension Eleven Human Resources and Communications

"I am pleased to recommend Bob 'Idea Man' Hooey to any organization looking for a charismatic, confident speaker and seminar leader. I have seen Bob in action on several occasions, and he is ALWAYS on!

Bob has the ability to grab his audience's attention and keep it. Quite simply, if Bob is involved - your program or seminar is guaranteed to succeed." **Maurice Laving**, Coordinator Training and Development, London Drugs

"On very short notice Bob cleared his schedule and graciously presented at our meeting when the original Speaker was unable to attend. **Last week Bob set the tone for our two-day BMO leadership meeting and gave us all a motivational lift.** *His compassion and true interest in people was clearly evident, making him very credible. He shared some great stories, has a wealth of experience and knowledge and it was a pleasure listening to him. His down-to-Earth style makes it easier to retain the information presented. He also followed up with additional info and handouts, cementing his message of building bridges, not walls. Fantastic job, Bob, and thanks again!"* **Barbara Afra Beler**, MBA, Senior Specialist Commercial Community, Alberta North

Growth is based on a seed planted with care!

*"**I have been so excited working with Bob Hooey**, as he has given inspiration and motivation to our leadership team members. Both at the Brick Warehouse – Alberta and at Art Van Furniture – Michigan; with his years of experience in working with business executives and his humorous and delightful packaging of his material, he makes **learning with Bob a real joy**. But most importantly, anyone who encounters his material is the better for it."*
Kim Yost, retired CEO Art Van Furniture, former CEO The Brick

Motivate your teams, your employees, and your leaders to 'productively' grow and 'profitably' succeed!

Protect your conference investment - leverage your training dollars.

Enhance your professional career and sell more products and services.

Equip and motivate your leaders and their teams to grow and succeed, 'even' in tough times!

Leverage your time to enhance your skills, equip your teams, and better serve your clients.

Leverage your leadership and investment of time to leave a significant legacy!

*"**Sales are contingent upon the attitude of the salesman – not the attitude of the prospect.**"* **W. Clement Stone**

Bob's Publications

Bob is a prolific author who has been capturing and sharing his wisdom and experience in printed and electronic forms for the past twenty plus years. In addition to the following publications he has written for consumer, corporate, professional associations, trade, and on-line publications. He has also been engaged to write and assist on publications by other writers and companies.

Leadership, business, and career development series

Running TOO Fast (8th edition 2019)
Legacy of Leadership (3rd edition 2019)
Make ME Feel Special! (6th edition 2019)
Why Didn't I 'THINK' of That? (5th edition 2019)
Speaking for Success! (9th edition 2020)
THINK Beyond the First Sale (3rd edition 2019)
Prepare Yourself to Win! (3rd edition 2017)
The early years… 1998-2009 – A Tip of the Hat collection (2020)
The saga continues… 2010-2019 - A Tip of the Hat collection (2020)

Bob's Mini-book success series

The Courage to Lead! (4th edition 2017)
Creative Conflict (3rd edition 2017)
THINK Before You Ink! (3rd edition 2017)
Running to Win! (2nd edition 2017)

How to Generate More Sales (4th edition 2017)
Unleash your Business Potential (3rd edition 2017)
Maximize Meetings (2019)
Learn to Listen (2nd edition 2017)
Creativity Counts! (2nd edition 2016)
Create Your Future! (3rd edition 2017)

Bob's Pocket Wisdom series

Pocket Wisdom for Speakers (updated 2019)
Pocket Wisdom for Leaders – Power of One! (2019)

Quick reads (2017-2020) - more in 2020

LEAD! *Idea-rich leadership success strategies*
CREATE! *Idea-rich strategies for enhanced innovation*
TIME! *Idea-rich tips for enhanced performance and productivity*
SERVE! *Idea-rich strategies for enhanced customer service*
SPEAK! *Idea-rich tips and techniques for great presentations*
CREATIVE CONFLICT *Idea-rich leadership for team success*
SUCCEED! *Idea-rich strategies to succeed in business, despite global disruptions (2020)*
WRITE ON! *Idea-rich tips and techniques to bring your book into pixels or print (2020)*
Get to Yes! *Idea-rich introductions to subtle art of creative persuasion in sales and negotiation (2020)*

Co-authored books created by Bob

Quantum Success – 3 volume series (2006)
In the Company of Leaders (95th anniversary Edition 2019)
Foundational Success (2nd Edition 2013)

Visit: www.SuccessPublications.ca for more information

Copyright and License Notes

Get to YES!
Idea-rich introductions to the subtle art of creative persuasion in sales and negotiation

Bob 'Idea Man' Hooey, Accredited Speaker, 2011 Spirit of CAPS recipient. Prolific author of 30 plus business, leadership, and career success publications. Author, Think Beyond The FIRST Sale

Unattributed quotations are by Bob 'Idea Man' Hooey

Photos of Bob: Bonnie-Jean McAllister,
www.elantraphotography.com
Dov Friedman, www.photographybyDov.com
Editorial, layout and design: **Irene Gaudet,** Vitrak Creative Services, vitrakcreative.com

Success Publications – a division of Creativity Corner Inc.
Box 10, Egremont, AB T0A 0Z0 www.successpublications.ca
Creative office: +1-780-736-0009

Acknowledgements, warnings, and disclaimers

A very special dedication of this piece of myself, to the two people who meant the most to me, my folks Ron and Marge Hooey. Sadly, both my parents left this earthly realm in 1999. I still miss your encouragement and love. I was blessed with the two of you in my life.

*To my amazing wife and professional proof-reader, **Irene,** who loves, encourages, and supports me in my quest to continue sharing my **Ideas At Work!** across the world. Thank you seems so inadequate for your work in helping make my writing better!*

My thanks to the many people who have encouraged me in my growth as a leader, speaker, and engaging trainer in each area of expertise including sales and negotiation. My thanks to a select few friends for your ongoing support and constructive abuse. ☺ You know who you are.

We have not attempted to cite in the electronic text all the authorities and sources consulted in the preparation of this manual. To do so would require much more space than is available. The list would include departments of various governments, libraries, industrial institutions, periodicals, and many individuals. Inspiration was drawn from many sources in the creation of this electronic text.

Warning—Disclaimer

This electronic book is written and designed to provide information on more effective sales and negotiation. It is sold with the explicit understanding that the publisher and author are <u>not</u> engaged in rendering legal, accounting, or other professional services. If legal or other expert assistance is required, the services of a competent professional in your geographic area should be sought.
It is not the purpose of this electronic book (manual) to reprint all the information that is otherwise available to sales professionals, negotiators, and sales leaders. Its primary purpose is to complement, amplify, and supplement other texts and reference materials. You are encouraged to search out and study all the available material, learn as much as possible, and tailor the information

to your individual needs. This will help to enhance your success in being a more effective sales leader, negotiator, or sales professional.

*Every effort has been made to make this electronic 'primer' as complete and as accurate as possible within the scope of its focus. However, there **may be mistakes**, both typographical and in content. Therefore, this electronic text should be used only as a general guide or primer and not as the ultimate source of information. Furthermore, this electronic manual contains information that is current only up to the date of publication.*

The purpose of this electronic 'primer' is to educate and entertain; perhaps to inform and to inspire. The author and/or publisher shall have <u>neither</u> liability <u>nor</u> responsibility to any person or entity with respect to any loss or damage caused, or alleged to have been caused, directly or indirectly, by the information contained in this electronic 'primer' manual or electronic book.

If you do not wish to be bound by the above, you may return this book to the publisher for a full refund.

**Getting to YES! Starts with a proper mindset and
is anchored on solid commitments**

Thanks for purchasing and reading Get to YES!

Each time I sit down to write, or in this case to re-write, I am challenged to ensure I deliver something that will be of use-it-now value to my reader.

- I ask myself, **"If I was reading this, what would I be looking for?"**
- As well as, **"Why is this relevant to me, today?"**

These two questions help to keep me focused, help me to remain clear on my objectives; and they help to remind me to dig into my experiences, stories, examples, and research to provide solid information that will be of benefit and help my readers, when they apply it, succeed. That can be an exciting challenge!

I trust I have done that for you in this updated primer on more effective sales and negotiation. **Get to YES!** is my attempt to capture some of the valuable lessons learned over the past 25 plus years and to share them with you.

I'd love to hear from you and read your success stories. If you would be so kind, please drop me a quick email at: bob@ideaman.net

Bob 'Idea Man' Hooey
http://www.ideaman.net
http://www.SuccessPublications.ca
http://www.HaveMouthWillTravel.com

Connect with me on:
Facebook: http://www.facebook.com/bob.hooey
LinkedIn: www.linkedin.com/in/canadianideamanbobhooey

YouTube: www.youtube.com/ideamanbob
Smashwords: www.smashwords.com/profile/view/Hooey

Bob speaking in Paris, France

Call today to engage author, award winning, inspirational leadership keynote speaker, leaders' success coach, and employee development trainer, **Bob 'Idea Man' Hooey** and his innovative, audience based, results-focused, **Ideas At Work!** for your next company, convention, leadership, staff, training, or association event. You'll be glad you did!

Bob can present live or in a virtual format to assist you and your team in their growth and ongoing success.

Call +1-780-736-0009 to connect with Bob 'Idea Man' Hooey today!

Email: bhooey@mcsnet.ca
Learn more about Bob at: **www.ideaman.net** or **www.BobHooey.training**

www.ingramcontent.com/pod-product-compliance
Lightning Source LLC
Chambersburg PA
CBHW070318160726
47999CB00003B/1074